First World War
and Army of Occupation
War Diary
France, Belgium and Germany

39 DIVISION
Divisional Troops
Divisional Trench Mortar Batteries
3 July 1916 - 20 July 1918

WO95/2574/6

The Naval & Military Press Ltd
www.nmarchive.com
Published in association with The National Archives

Published by

The Naval & Military Press Ltd

Unit 10 Ridgewood Industrial Park,

Uckfield, East Sussex,

TN22 5QE England

Tel: +44 (0) 1825 749494

www.naval-military-press.com

www.nmarchive.com

This diary has been reprinted in facsimile from the original. Any imperfections are inevitably reproduced and the quality may fall short of modern type and cartographic standards.

© Crown Copyright
Images reproduced by permission of The National Archives, London, England, 2015.

Contents

Document type	Place/Title	Date From	Date To
Heading	WO95/2574 July 16-July 18 39 Div Div Trench Mortar Batteries		
Heading	Trench Mortar Batteries Jly 1916-Jly 1918		
Heading	X.Y.Z. 39th Medium Trench Mortar Brigade July 1916 Jul 1918		
War Diary		03/07/1916	31/07/1916
Heading	39th Divisional Trench Mortar Brigade (X.Y.Z. Batteries) & "V" Heavy Btty. August 1916		
War Diary	Field	18/08/1916	31/08/1916
Heading	39 Div A C Vol I		
Heading	39th Divisional Trench Mortar Brigade (X.Y.Z. Batteries) & "V" Heavy Batty; ; September 1916		
War Diary		01/09/1916	26/09/1916
Heading	39th Divisional Trench Mortar Brigade ("V" Heavy & X,Y,Z Medium) October 1916		
Miscellaneous	D.A.G. 3rd Echelon Base.	09/11/1916	09/11/1916
War Diary		01/10/1916	25/10/1916
Heading	39th Divisional Trench Mortar Brigade ("V" Heavy & X,Y & Z Medium) November 1916		
War Diary		01/11/1916	25/11/1916
Heading	39th Divisional Trench Mortar Brigade ("V" Heavy & X,Y & Z Medium) December 1916		
War Diary		04/09/1916	31/07/1917
Heading	Headquarters 39th Divisional T.M. Bty War Diary 1-8-1917 To 31-8 1917		
War Diary		03/08/1917	02/11/1917
Miscellaneous	War Diary December 1917		
War Diary		01/12/1917	31/03/1918
Heading	39th Divisional Trench Mortars April 1918		
War Diary		01/04/1918	18/05/1918
War Diary	St. Leger	02/07/1918	02/07/1918
War Diary	Drooglandt.	03/07/1918	03/07/1918
War Diary	St Janter Biezen	18/07/1918	20/07/1918

7

WO95/2574

July '16 – July '18
39 Div.
Div. Trench Mortar Batteries

39TH DIVISION
DIVL ARTILLERY

TRENCH MORTAR BATTERIES

JLY 1916-JLY 1918

39th Divisional Artillery.

24

"X.Y.Z." 39th MEDIUM TRENCH MORTAR BRIGADE

JULY 1916

X/39, 1/39 and 2/39 Medium Trench Mortar Batteries

WAR DIARY or **SECRET INTELLIGENCE SUMMARY**

From 1st to 31st July 1916

Army Form C. 2118

Volume I. Vol I

39

Place	Date	Hour	Summary of Events and Information	Remarks and references to Appendices
	July 3rd		X/39 Bty transferred from Ferme du Bois Section to Givenchy Section	
	5th		X/39 cooperated with Artillery & MTMs of 33rd Div in bombardment of Northern Craters, Givenchy, in support of an assault by 19th Infantry Bde on enemy trenches	
	6th		Half of X/39 transferred from Givenchy to Auchy Section under the orders of 33rd Div.	
	7th		X/39 came under the orders of 39th Div	
	8th		1/39 transferred from Ferme du Bois to Givenchy Section	
			2/39 do	
	10th		Half of X/39 withdrawn from Auchy Section to Gorre	
	11th		1/39 cut gap in enemy wire at Quinque Rue crossing preparatory to a raid by 17th Infantry Bde.	
	16th		Decorations awarded: Military Medal, 61327 Sgt Knibbs RHA, 2/39 no 40632 Gnr Crooks RGA, X/39.	
	17th		X/39, 1/39 & 2/39 bombarded Northern Craters & Duck's Bill, Givenchy in co-operation with Divisional Artillery	
			2Lt E. Sierrar RA O.C. 1/39 wounded.	
			2Lt F. Straker RFA. 2/39, wounded & died of wounds	
			2Lt R C Rodger RFA, from X/39, took command of 1/39 vice 2Lt Straker.	
	18th		1/39 fired on Crater Trench Givenchy in support of raid by 118th Infantry Bde	
	19th		2Lt Hallington from B/179 attached to 2/39 vice 2Lt Straker.	
	20th			

WAR DIARY or INTELLIGENCE SUMMARY

Army Form C. 2118

Place	Date	Hour	Summary of Events and Information	Remarks and references to Appendices
	July 21st		Decorations awarded: Military Medal, 101386 C/L G. Richards R.F.A. L33496 Gnr G.R. Iles R.F.A, Y/39, Bomb. G. Cutts (L31864 R.F.A.) Z/39 and Gnr W. Croxon (59607 R.F.A.) X/39.	
	22nd		Decoration awarded: Military Cross, 2Lt (temp Capt) O.C.K. Corrie North Somerset Yeomanry, Divisional T.M. Officer.	
	21st 22nd		Y/39 cut gaps in wire in front of CRATER Trench Givenchy, preliminary to raid by 118th Infantry Bde.	
	23rd		Lt J.N. Young R.F.A. from A/174 attacked to X/39 vice 2Lt R.C. Rodger Lt J.E. Sierra R.F.A. (Y/39).	
	28th		Decoration awarded: Military Cross, 2Lt J.E. Sierra R.F.A. (Y/39).	
	29th 30th 31st		X/39, Y/39 & Z/39 cut gaps in enemy's wire preliminary to raid on Ducks Bill by 117th Inf Bde.	
	31st		X/39 & Z/39 bombarded enemy's trenches in co-operation with attack, in support of raiding party of 117th Inf Bde.	

M Mee Capt.
TMO 39th Div.

39th Divisional Artillery,

39th DIVISIONAL TRENCH MORTAR BRIGADE

(X. Y. Z. Batteries)
& "V" Heavy Btty.

AUGUST 1916

39th Division Trench Mortar Batteries   August 1916   Army Form C. 2118

WAR DIARY
or
INTELLIGENCE SUMMARY
(Erase heading not required.)

Place	Date	Hour	Summary of Events and Information	Remarks and references to Appendices
Field	Aug 1. 18th		X/39, Y/39 & Z/39 Batteries located at ST MICHEL-EN-TERNOISE. 2 Lt Follit R.F.A., Z/39 Battery, struck off the strength of 39th Div Arty on posting to R.F.C.	
	27th		X/39, Y/39 & Z/39 proceeded to LUCHEUX. X/39, Y/39 & Z/39 proceeded to THIEVRES. X/39, Y/39 & Z/39 proceeded to BUS-EN-ARTOIS. Y/39 Heavy T.M. Battery formed on arrival at Bus-en-Artois, personnel housed at 3rd Army School of Mortars. Lt G. O. C. Prosser R.F.A. transferred from Z/39 to Y/39.	
	31st		Lt T. Aukusan R.F.A. transferred from X/39 to Y/39. 2 Lt A. J. C. Fyfe R.F.A. attached to X/39. 2 Lt C. M. Mortimer R.F.A. attached to Y/39.	

C W Morris Capt
TMO 39 Divn.

39th Division Trench Mortar Battery August 1916 Army Form C. 2118

WAR DIARY or INTELLIGENCE SUMMARY

Place	Date	Hour	Summary of Events and Information	Remarks and references to Appendices
Field	Aug 1 18th		X/39, Y/39, Z/39 Batteries located at ST MICHEL-EN-TERNOISE. 2 Lt. FOLLIT R.F.A., Z/39 Battery, struck off the strength of 39th Div Arty on posting to R.F.C. X/39, Y/39, Z/39 proceeded to LUCHEUX. X/39, Y/39 & Z/39 proceeded to THIEVRES. X/39, Y/39 & Z/39 proceeded to BUS-EN-ARTOIS.	
	27th		V/39 Heavy T.M. Battery formed on arrival at BUS-EN-ARTOIS of personnel trained at 3rd Army School of Mortars. Lt. G.O.C. PROBERT R.G.A. transferred from Z/39 to V/39 Lt. T MULLIGAN R.F.A. transferred from X/39 to V/39	
	31st		2 Lt A.J.C. FYFE R.F.A. attached to X/39 2 Lt. C.M. MORTIMER R.F.A. attached to Y/39	

T.W. Orrin Capt.
TMO 39 Div.

39 Dw
AC
Vol 1

39th Divisional Artillery.

39th DIVISIONAL ~~OBDOOR~~ TRENCH MORTAR BRIGADE

(X. Y. Z. Batteries)
& "V" Heavy Btty;;
SEPTEMBER 1 9 1 6

WAR DIARY

INTELLIGENCE SUMMARY

54th Division Trench Mortar Battery — September 1916

Army Form C. 2118

(Erase heading not required.)

Place	Date	Hour	Summary of Events and Information	Remarks and references to Appendices
	1st		Y/139, X/139, Y/139 & Z/139 located at ENGLEBELMER	
	2nd		2/Lt/ E. H. P. THOMPSON RFA transferred from Y/139 to Y/139.	
	4th		Y/139, X/139, Y/139 & Z/139 relieved Y/29, X/29, Y/29, Z/29 & S/29 respectively in BEAUMONT HAMEL Section.	
	8th		Lt-Col. C. PROBERT RGA struck off strength of Y/139 on transfer to Do K Heavy Battery.	
	26th		M M Battery fires in co-operation with Divisional Artillery in support of attack by Division operating South from ANCRE. Rounds fired — Medium 505, heavy 52.	

M Munroe Capt
TMO 39 Div"

39th Division Trench Mortar Batteries

War Diary

1st September 1916.

1st   X/39, Y/39, 1/39 & 2/39 located at ENGLEBELMER.
  "   2 Lt / E H P THOMPSON RFA transferred from 1/39 to Y/39.
4th   Y/39, X/39, 1/39 & 2/39 relieved Y/29, X/29, 1/29 & 2/29 & 5/29
       respectively in BEAUMONT HAMEL Section.
       1/Lt — C PRESCOTT RGA struck off strength of 1/39 on transfer
8th   to 120th Heavy Battery.
26th   All Batteries fired in co-operation with Divisional Artillery in support
       of attack by Division operating south of River ANCRE. Rounds fired —
       medium 505, heavy 52.

M H Moore Capt
TMO 39 Divn

39th Divisional Artillery.

39th DIVISIONAL TRENCH MORTER BRIGADE

("V" Heavy & X,Y,Z Medium)

OCTOBER 1 9 1 6

SECRET & CONFIDENTIAL.

D.A.G.,
　　3rd Echelon,
　　　　BASE.

　　　　Herewith War Diaries for the month of October, in continuation of my 39/1197/A dated 4.11.16., as follows :-

　　　　V/39. Heavy T.M.Battery.
　　　　X/39 Medium T.M.Battery.
　　　　Y/39　　"　　　"
　　　　Z/39　　"　　　"

Please acknowledge receipt.

　　　　　　　　　　　　　　　　　Major-General.
9.11.16.　　　　　　　Commanding 39th Division.

Trench Mortar Batteries of 39th Division   October 1916.

WAR DIARY
INTELLIGENCE SUMMARY
Vol: 1.

SECRET

Army Form C. 2118

Place	Date	Hour	Summary of Events and Information	Remarks and references to Appendices
	1st		V/39, X/39, Y/39 and Z/39 Batteries in action in BEAUMONT HAMEL Sector.	
	12th		2 Lt E.S. Wise R.F.A, 39th T.M.A.C. attached to V/39.	
	15th		2/39 in co-operation with 2/1 T.M Battery, carried out a bombardment of Y Ravine with gas bombs.	
	20th		V/39, X/39, Y/39 and Z/39 came under the orders of G.O.C. 63rd Div. Arty.	
	21st		2/39 withdrawn from AUCHONVILLERS Sub-Section.	
	23rd		2 Lt E.S. Wise R.F.A. W/39, wounded (gas poisoning)	

C.T Cormie Capt.
T.M.o 39 Division.

39th Divisional Artillery.

39th DIVISIONAL TRENCH MORTAR BRIGADE

("V" Heavy & X,Y & Z Medium)

NOVEMBER 1916

39th Division Trench Mortars Battn.

WAR DIARY
or
INTELLIGENCE SUMMARY

Army Form C. 2118

1/30 November 1916. Vol 5

Place	Date	Hour	Summary of Events and Information	Remarks and references to Appendices
	Nov 6		Y/39, X/39, 1/39, 2/39 in action in BEAUMONT HAMEL Sector	
	12		X/39, Y/39, 2/39 engaged in cutting enemy's front line wire.	
	13		Y/39, X/39 and 1/39 & 2/39 fired in support of assault by 63rd (R.N) Division on enemy's trenches.	
	16		Y/39 & 2/39 how.M mortars into action in captured trench near BEAUCOURT.	
	18		Y/39 & 2/39 in support of attack by 37th Division	
	19		2D.M.S.M. for Middley Rept. after fight at Y/39. FKMK for T. trench near BEAUCOURT. A.A. Batteries withdrawn from R2 to ENGLEBELMER	
	20		M Battery entrained at ACHEUX, noter transport	
	23		All Batteries arrived at POPERINGHE, 39th Division	
	25		M Battery proceeded to HOUTKERQUE	

Christie Capt

TMB 39 Div.

39th Divisional Artillery.

39th DIVISIONAL TRENCH MORTAR BRIGADE

("V" Heavy & X, Y & Z Medium)

DECEMBER 1916.

Trench Mortar Batteries of 39th Division December 1916   Vol #D 6

WAR DIARY
INTELLIGENCE SUMMARY

Place	Date	Hour	Summary of Events and Information	Remarks and references to Appendices
	4th		Y/39 came under the orders of 38th Division & went into action in the BOESINGHE Sector.	
	14th		Y/39 came under orders of 39th Division.	
	"		X/39, Z/39 & V/39 went into action in YPRES SALIENT LEFT.	
			relieving Batteries of 38th Division.	
	20th		2Lt N.M. DOBSON, Middlesex Regt attached V/39, No 15 to X/39.	
	"		2Lt B.O.E. WALPOLE RFA attached to Y/39.	
	"		2Lt A.M. PRATT R.F.A attached to Y/39.	
	"		2Lt A.B. HARPER R.F.A attached to Z/39.	

M.Comie cept
TMB 39 Div.
1.1.17

39th Division French Mortar Battery   WAR DIARY   January 1917   Army Form C. 2118

INTELLIGENCE SUMMARY

Vol 7

Place	Date	Hour	Summary of Events and Information	Remarks and references to Appendices
	1st		Batteries in action, Y/39 in BOESINGHE, X/39, Z/39 & V/39 in YPRES Salient Left. 2/Lt F.V. WALLINGTON R.F.A. 2/39, posted to Divisional Artillery. 2/Lt A. ROBERTSON R.F.A. from Divisional Artillery posted to X/39. 2/Lt A.J.C. FYFE (X/39) R.F.A. posted to 55th Division.	
	"			
	18th		X/39, Y/39, Z/39 & V/39 relieved by Batteries of 38th Division & went into Ypres / YPRES Salient Sector, relieving Batteries of 55th Division.	

T C Moore
Capt
TMO 39 Div ?

39th Division Trench Mortar Batteries

WAR DIARY
—or—
INTELLIGENCE SUMMARY

February 1917. Army Form C. 2118

Vol 8

Place	Date	Hour	Summary of Events and Information	Remarks and references to Appendices
	1st		Batteries in action in YPRES SALIENT (RAILWAY WOOD Sector)	M Morris Capt. DW T.M Officer 39
	2nd 11th		X/39, Y/39 & Z/39 co-operated with divisional Heavy Artillery in cutting enemy's front line wire.	
	18th		Batteries were relieved by T.M. Batteries of 55th Division & proceeded to POPERINGHE.	
	19th		Batteries proceeded to HOUTKERQUE.	
	27th		Batteries relieved T.M Batteries of 23rd Division in YPRES SALIENT (SANCTUARY WOOD Sector)	

39 Divisional Trench Mortar Batteries

Army Form C. 2118

WAR DIARY
~~INTELLIGENCE~~ SUMMARY
(Erase heading not required.)

for March 1917

Vol 9

Instructions regarding War Diaries and Intelligence Summaries are contained in F. S. Regs., Part II. and the Staff Manual respectively. Title Pages will be prepared in manuscript.

Place	Date	Hour	Summary of Events and Information	Remarks and references to Appendices
	March		Trench Mortar Batteries in Action in YPRES SALIENT. SANCTUARY WOOD SECTOR.	
	12		Lieutenant R.G. Rodger M.C. R.F.A. Y/39 Posted to Royal Flying Corps. 2nd Lieutenant E.M. Mortimer R.F.A. to command Y/39 vice Lieutenant R.G. Rodger, and to be Acting Lieutenant dated 12/3/17. Lieutenant J.W. Young R.F.A. X/39 Posted to "C" 189 Army Field Artillery Brigade R.F.A. 2nd Lieutenant W.M. Dobson 39th Middlesex Regiment (T.F.) to command X/39 vice Lieutenant J.W. Young to be Acting Lieutenant dated 21/3/17	
	21st		2nd Lieutenant B.O.E. Walpole V/39 Heavy T.M. Battery Posted to 39th D.A.C. with effect from 21/3/1917. 2nd Lieutenant P.R. Ambrose Essex Regiment (T.F.) attached 1st Herts Regiment, attached to Y/39 for experience.	Captain Officer m/ Monie Trench Mortar 39 Div

39th Divisional Trench Mortar Batt. WAR DIARY for April 1917. Army Form C. 2118

INTELLIGENCE SUMMARY
(Erase heading not required.)

1 of 10

Place	Date	Hour	Summary of Events and Information	Remarks and references to Appendices
	1st		V/39, X/39, Y/39, Z/39, in action in Sanctuary Wood Sector.	
	7th		Y/39 in action in Hill 60 Sector in co-operation with 47th Divl Arty. (Smoke Barrage covering a daylight raid).	
	9th		V/39, X/39, Z/39 withdrawn to Reserve Area, HERZEELE	
	16th		Y/39 withdrawn to Herzeele.	
	17th		2/Lt. Am. Pratt rejoined from Base.	
	30th		V/39, X/39, Y/39, Z/39, into Wieltje Sector	

O.R. Connor
Capt.
TMO 39 Divn

39th Division Trench Mortar Batteries WAR DIARY for May 1917

Army Form C. 2118

INTELLIGENCE SUMMARY

(Erase heading not required.)

Vol XI

Place	Date	Hour	Summary of Events and Information	Remarks and references to Appendices
	2nd 5/17		V/39, X/39, Y/39, and Z/39 Trench Mortar Batteries commenced work on Medium and Heavy T.M. emplacements.	
	3rd 5/17		Work on pits suspended. Daily party of 2 officers and 70 ORs employed on cable digging for R.E. Signals.	
	11th 5/17		2/Lt. R.L. Close joined 39th Div T.M. Batteries and posted to Z/39 MTMBty.	
	"		2/Lt U.M. Pratt attached Y/39 M.T.M. Battery posted to 39th R.A.C.	
	12th 5/17		2/Lt A.D. Hatter attached Z/39 M.T.M. Battery posted to Royal Flying Corps	
	14-15th 5/17		On night of 14th–15th X/39 T.M. Battery in action at Cross Roads Farm in support of raid by 118th Infantry Brigade.	
	20th 5/17		Captain O.C.K. Corrie M.C. Divisional Trench Mortar Officer posted to 3rd Army School of Mortars and ceased to hold command of 39th Division Trench Mortar Batteries.	
	30th 5/17		Cable digging for R.E. Signals finished, work on gun pits resumed.	

J. McGuigan, Captain R.F.A.
D.T.M.O. 39 Dn

39 Div'l T.M Batteries

39D TM By
for June 1917
Jot 1 2

WAR DIARY
or
INTELLIGENCE SUMMARY
(Erase heading not required.)

Army Form C. 2118

Place	Date	Hour	Summary of Events and Information	Remarks and references to Appendices
	30th May 1st June		Lt. W.M. Dobson 3/9 Middlesex Regt (TF) attached to X/39 Medium Trench Mortar Battery granted ten days leave to England, period of leave 30/5/17 to 9/6/17.	
	1st to 3rd		Y/39 Medium Trench Mortar Battery engaged on construction of Trench mortar emplacements in Hilltop Sector Wieltje Sub-section	
	3rd		X/39 Medium Trench Mortar Battery in action at Crow Roads Farm under the command of Lieut JA Proctor in support of VIII Corps demonstration.	
	6th		2/Lieut (a/Capt) Mulligan RFA appointed Divisional Trench Mortar Officer 39th Division with effect from 21-5-17 vice 2/Lt (a/Capt) AGT Corrie to Third Army Trench mortar school.	
	7th		Demonstration by VIII Corps in support of assaults by Southern Army. X/39 Medium Trench mortar Battery in action at Crow Road Farm	
	8th		2/Lt Wise ES 39th Divisional Ammunition Column posted to X/39 Medium Trench Mortar Battery. 2/Lt Robertson A. X/39 Medium Trench Mortar Battery posted to "B" Battery 186th Brigade RFA.	
	12th		2/Lt (a/C) CM Mortimer attached Y/39 Medium Trench Mortar Battery posted to Royal Flying Corps as observer.	
	13th		39th Division left the VIII Corps, 2nd Army, and came under the orders of the XVIII Corps, 5th Army, X y Z/39 Medium Trench Mortar Batteries engaged in construction of new emplacements in Hill Top Sub-section. 2/Lt Wale A. Y/39 Medium Trench Mortar Battery proceeded on ten days leave to England.	

Y/39

WAR DIARY
—or—
INTELLIGENCE SUMMARY for June 1917 (Cont)

(Erase heading not required.)

Army Form C. 2118

Place: 39th Divnl. T.M. Batteries

Instructions regarding War Diaries and Intelligence Summaries are contained in F.S. Regs., Part II. and the Staff Manual respectively. Title Pages will be prepared in manuscript.

Place	Date	Hour	Summary of Events and Information	Remarks and references to Appendices
	11th		Y/39 Medium Trench Mortar Battery relieved in Wulfge Sub-section by 55th Division.	
			39th Division relieved 30th Division in Lancashire Farm Sub-section.	
	21st		2/Lt. P.R. Ambrose of/39 Medium Trench Mortar Battery granted ten days leave to England period of leave 21-6-17 to 1-7-17.	
			39th Division relieved by 51st (Highland) Division in Lancashire Farm Sub-section.	
			The casualties for the month ended 30th June 1917 have been greater than due to any corresponding period in the history of the 39th Divisional Trench Mortar Batteries.	

J. Mulligan.
Capt. R.F.A.
D.T.M.O. 39th Div.

WAR DIARY
INTELLIGENCE SUMMARY

39th Divisional Trench Mortar Batteries for July 1917.

Vol / 3

Army Form C. 2118

Place	Date	Hour	Summary of Events and Information	Remarks and references to Appendices
	8th		48th Divisional Trench Mortar Batteries take over sector covered by "Left Group R.A."	
	14th		2/Lt. W.J. Horner R.G.A. attached to V/39 Heavy Trench Mortar Battery wounded (shellfire)	
	15th		2/Lt. W.J. Horner R.G.A. attached to V/39 H.T.M. Batty Died of Wounds at No.10 CCS	
	20th		2. 6" Trench Mortars of 39th Division and one of 48th Division commenced wire cutting along Divisional Front.	
	22nd & 25th		Wire cutting continued by all 2" and 6" Trench Mortars of 39th & 48th Division	
	26th		Wire cutting continued by all 2" and 6" Trench Mortars of 39th & 48th Division and wire cutting with 1-9.45 Trench Mortar (V-39) in action against HAMPSHIRE FARM.	
	27th & 30th		Wire cutting continued by all 2" and 6" Trench Mortars of 39th & 48th Divisions.	
	31st		Fifth Army attacked and captured enemy trench system E & N.E. of YPRES. Battle casualties for month — 1 Officer died of wounds 1 O.R. killed in action 10 ,, ,, ,, ,, 15 ORs. Wounded in action	

E. J. Mucipa. Capt. R.A.
3rd DTMB

Vol 14 *Confidential*

Headquarters
39th Divisional ~~Artillery~~ T.M. Bty.

War Diary

1-8-1917 to 31-8-1917

Army Form C. 2118

WAR DIARY
or
INTELLIGENCE SUMMARY

39ᵗʰ Divnl. Trench Mortar Batteries

August 1917

(Erase heading not required.)

Place	Date	Hour	Summary of Events and Information	Remarks and references to Appendices
	3rd	—	40 men of 39ᵗʰ Divisional Trench Mortar Batteries attached to 240ᵗʰ Brigade Royal Field Artillery (48ᵗʰ Division)	
	6ᵗʰ		39ᵗʰ Division less R.A., R.E. and Pioneers relieved by 48ᵗʰ Division Command of front passed to G.O.C. 48ᵗʰ Division	

J. Sweetjar.
Capt R.F.A.
D.T.M.O. 39 Dn.

Army Form C. 2118.

39th Divis. Trench Mortar Batteries

WAR DIARY
or
INTELLIGENCE SUMMARY.

(Erase heading not required.)

September 1917

Vol 15

Place	Date	Hour	Summary of Events and Information	Remarks and references to Appendices
	4th		Lt. J.E. Thompson granted 10 days leave to England	
	10th		21 men of 39th Divnl Trench Mortar Batteries attached to 39th Div. L.G. Rein	A/186 Bde Rest
				C/186
	12th		" " " "	
	15th		Capt Col. L. Johnston granted 10 days leave to England	
	21st		The above detailed men rejoined unit.	
	28th		Capt Mulligan T. granted 10 days leave to England.	
	30th		Relieds handed over to 5th Divn T.M. Batteries	
			9.45 T.Howz & 6 in Newton T.Howz taken over by 39th Divnl T.M. Batteries	
			Casualties for month — Killed 2 O.R.	
			Wounded 3 O.R.	

P.F. Ambrose Lieut
for O.C. 39 Divn
T.M.B.

39 Div TRENCH MORTAR BATTERIES. **WAR DIARY** October 1917. Army Form C. 2118.

INTELLIGENCE SUMMARY
(Erase heading not required.)

Vol 16

Place	Date	Hour	Summary of Events and Information	Remarks and references to Appendices
	1st to 8th		Personnel of 39th Divisional Trench Mortar Batteries attached to 174th Brigade as reinforcements for artillery.	
	8th		39th Divisional Trench Mortar Batteries withdrawn to Merris area on 8th inst.	
	25th		39th Divisional Trench Mortar Batteries proceeded to Westoutre Area under orders of 39th Divisional artillery	
	28th to 31st		39th Divisional Trench Mortar Batteries engaged on building Medium and Heavy Trench Mortar emplacements in Tower Hamlets sector	

J M ?
Capt R.A.
D.T.M.O.
39 Div

39th Div TRENCH MORTAR BATTERIES WAR DIARY

Army Form C. 2118.

39D TM 8/5
Nov. 1917
Vol 17

INTELLIGENCE SUMMARY.
(Erase heading not required.)

Place	Date	Hour	Summary of Events and Information	Remarks and references to Appendices
	1st to 30th		39th Divisional Trench Mortar Batteries employed on salvage duties and assisted 39th Divisional Artillery in action.	
	22nd Nov.		39th Divisional Trench Mortar Batteries engaged on putting 2 six inch newton and 1 9.45" Trench Mortar in action in Gheluvelt Sector	

J Murray
Capt RFA
DTMO
39 Div

Confidential

39 DTM By
Ⅹ⎯18

Hed. Divt. Artillery

War Diary

December 1917.

3/ Divisional Train Horses Batteries December 1915. Army Form C. 2118

WAR DIARY
or
INTELLIGENCE SUMMARY
(Erase heading not required.)

Army Form C. 2118

Instructions regarding War Diaries and Intelligence Summaries are contained in F. S. Regs., Part II. and the Staff Manual respectively. Title Pages will be prepared in manuscript.

Place	Date	Hour	Summary of Events and Information	Remarks and references to Appendices
	1st to 22nd		Batteries, horses exercising. Guns in Divnl. Rest. centre.	
	23rd to 28th		Batteries horses at rest in Toordspons area.	
	29th to 31st		18c Bty. attacked by H.E. shells and twenty five other ranks. Casualties for month. Killed 2 O.R. Wounded 1 O.R.	

J. McGuigan
Capt. R.H.
O.I./C. 3/ Divnl.

Army Form C. 2118.

39th Div TRENCH MORTAR WAR DIARY
BATTERIES INTELLIGENCE SUMMARY
for Jan 1919.

(Erase heading not required.)

Instructions regarding War Diaries and Intelligence Summaries are contained in F. S. Regs., Part II. and the Staff Manual respectively. Title pages will be prepared in manuscript.

Place	Date	Hour	Summary of Events and Information	Remarks and references to Appendices
	1st 15/16		Personnel of 39th Div Trench Mortar Batteries attached to 186th Bde R.F.A. as reinforcements.	
	3rd		39th Div Trench Mortar Batteries moved from NOORDEPENE artillery area to Ten Elms Camp PESELHOEK. Personnel of Batteries attached to 186 Bde RFA.	
	6th		39th Div Trench Mortar Batteries left Ten Elms Camp PESELHOEK and moved to Wamertinghe. Personnel of Batteries attached to 186 Bde RFA as reinforcements.	
	16th		Personnel of 39th Div Trench Mortar Batteries returned units and the whole of V/39 HTM Bty & X.Y.Z/39 M.T.M. Batteries moved from VLAMERTINGHE to REIGERSBERG CHATEAU. Personnel of V/39 Heavy T.M. Battery Annexed to 4th Army T.M. School on course of Instruction.	
Nt 28th			Personnel of X.Y.Z/39 Medium TM Batteries engaged on Barrage of Guns and ammunition in ST JULIEN wood sector.	
	25th			Personnel of X.Y.Z/39 Medium TM Batteries left REIGERSBERG Chateau and move to Ten Elms Camp PESELHOEK	
	28th			Personnel of X.Y.Z/39 Medium TM Batteries left Ten Elms Camp PESELHOEK for PROVEN STATION. Entraining at Proven Station for Marcourt La Abbe Somme area	
	29th			Personnel of X.Y.Z/39 Medium TM Batteries detrained at Marcourt La Abbe and marched to SAILLY LAURETTE SOMME remaining in Red Area until 31st	
1/2/1918				

J. M. William
Captain RA
D.T.M.B.
39 RA

39th Div Trench Mortar Batteries

Army Form C. 2118.

WAR DIARY
or
INTELLIGENCE SUMMARY

FEBRUARY 1918

Place	Date	Hour	Summary of Events and Information	Remarks and references to Appendices
	1st/2nd		X, Y, Z/39 Medium Trench Mortar Batteries at Rest at SAILLY LAURETTE, Corps Area SOMME	
	2nd		X, Y, Z/39 Medium Trench Mortar Batteries left SAILLY LAURETTE – on attachment to 9th and 21st Divisions in GOUZEAUCOURT SECTOR. 7/Lt E S Ware V/39 TMB posted to 2nd Army TM School	
	2nd		V/39 Heavy French Mortar Battery returned from course at 2nd Army TM School	
	3rd(?)/7th		X, Y, Z/39 Medium T.M. Batteries and V/39 Heavy TM Battery engaged on salvo of 6 pounder Hotchkiss guns from derelict Tanks in GOUZEAUCOURT SECTOR. Battery also engaged on construction of 6" mortar TM gun emplacements & mounting of salvaged 6 pounder guns.	
	7th		X, Y, Z/39 Medium Trench Mortar Batteries, V/39 Heavy Trench Mortar Battery reorganized and made 2–6" mortar Trench Mortar Batteries named X/39 Medium Trench Mortar Battery and Y/39 Medium Trench Mortar Battery.	
	7th to 15th		X/39 M T M Battery commanded this Battery – passed to Capt A Gradfield RFA and X/39 V Y/39 M T M Battery carried on work of construction	
	22nd		2/Lt B J Bavin RFA joined 39 Div TM Batteries from 39 Div R.F.A and failed to X/39 TMB	
			2/Lt W N France RFA joined 39 Div TM Batteries from 174 Bde and posted to Y/39 TMB	
			2/Lt T C Euliss RFA joined 39 Div TM Batteries from 186th Bde and posted to Y/39 TMB	
			2/Lt A J Applegate RFA joined 39 Div TM Battery from 186 Bde and posted to Y/39 TM	
	8th		2/Lt E S Martin (RGA) X/39 TM Bty posted to VII Corps H TMB	

J M Wilson
Cpt RA
D TMO 29

Place	Date	Summary
	1st to 9th	X/39 & Y/39 Medium Trench Mortar Batteries engaged in placing in position in GOUZEAUCOURT SECTOR, Six 6 Pounder Hotchkiss Anti-Tank Guns and Eight 6 and Nineteen 2" Newton T. Mortars and 16" Newton T. Mortars and laying a minefield on Divisional front. Thirty French Mortars.
	3rd	2/Lt. P. Newhall R.F.A. joined from Base and posted to Y/39 M.T.M. Battery.
	10th	X/39 and Y/39 Medium Trench Mortar Batteries withdrawn from line and relieved by T.M. Batteries of 9th and 21st Divisional Artilleries
	11th	X/39 and Y/39 Medium Trench Mortar Batteries moved from HEUDECOURT to PERONNE under orders from H.Q. 39th Div R.A.
	11th to 22nd	Batteries held in reserve at PERONNE
	23rd	Under orders from H.Q. 39th Div R.A. X/39 and Y/39 Medium Trench Mortar Batteries left PERONNE for CAPPY.
	24th	X/39 and Y/39 T.M. Batteries left CAPPY at 2am for BRAY-SUR-SOMME.
	25th	X/39 and Y/39 T.M. Batteries left BRAY-SUR-SOMME for PROYART
	26th	Batteries left PROYART at 12:0 M.D. for MORCOURT for CERISY. Batteries left MORCOURT at 5.0am Batteries left LE HAMEL for FOUILLOY
	27th	39 T.M. Batteries left CERISY for LE HAMEL, at 4.0pm Batteries left
	28th	X/39 and Y/39 T.M. Batteries left FOUILLOY for DOMART-SUR-LUCE
	30th	X/39 and Y/39. T.M. Batteries left DOMART-SUR-LUCE at 12.30pm for BOVES, at 4pm Batteries left BOVES for CAGNY.
	29th	A party of 14 other Ranks in charge of 2/Lt W.H. Pearce of X/39 M T M Battery reported missing Battle casualties
	21st	2/Lt. P. Newhall of X/39 M.T.M. B'y and 2 ORs wounded in action
	30-31	39 T.M. Batteries in reserve at CAGNY.

J.M. Weijen,
Capt RFA
D.T.M.O. 39 BA.

39th Divisional Artillery.

39th DIVISIONAL TRENCH MORTARS

APRIL 1918.

39ᵈ Div TRENCH MORTAR BATTERIES WAR DIARY   APRIL 1918   Army Form C. 2118.

INTELLIGENCE SUMMARY

(Erase heading not required.)

Place	Date	Hour	Summary of Events and Information	Remarks and references to Appendices
	12ᵗʰ		X/39 and Y/39 Medium Trench Mortar Batteries in reserve at BOUTILLERIE.	
	13ᵗʰ		X/39 and Y/39 M.T.M Batteries put in action 3.6" Newton Trench Mortars in HANGARD SECTOR	
	14ᵗʰ		Batteries relieved in HANGARD Sector by batteries of 61ˢᵗ Divisional Artillery	
	15ᵗʰ		Batteries left BOUTILLERIE and marched to BEHENCOURT under orders of H.Q. 39ᵗʰ Div R.A.	
	16ᵗʰ		X/39 - Y/39 M.T.M. Batteries left BEHENCOURT and marched under orders of 39ᵗʰ Div RA to SAULTY	
	17ᵗʰ 28ᵗʰ		Personnel of X/39 - Y/39 M.T.M Batteries at rest at SAULTY	
	29ᵗʰ		Personnel of X/39 - Y/39 M.T.M Batteries attached for duty to 174ᵗʰ Brigade and 186ᵗʰ Brigade R.F.A.	
	30ᵗʰ		Lieut (A/Capt) W.M Dobson Middlesex Regt attached 39ᵗʰ Divisional Artillery Medium Trench Mortar Batteries posted to 21ˢᵗ Battn Middlesex Regt 40ᵗʰ Division	

JW... Capt RFA
D.T.M.O
39...

39' Div Trench Mortar Batteries

WAR DIARY
or
INTELLIGENCE SUMMARY.

Army Form C. 2118.
May 1918
Vol 23

Place	Date	Hour	Summary of Events and Information	Remarks and references to Appendices
	1st to 6th		X/39, Y/39 Medium Trench Mortar Batteries in reserve at SAULTY. Personnel of these Batteries attached for duty to 17th & 186 Brigades RFA	
	7th & 8th		2nd Demobilization by Capt. J. Mulligan D.T.M.O. 39 RA. & for VI Corps RA commenced with 6" Mobile (Manned) Trench Mortar	
	15th		Under orders from H.Q. 39th Divl Artillery and 3rd Army Letter No M/A/1539/5 d/- 9-5-1918 the 39th Divisional Trench Mortar Batteries were disbanded & personnel being posted to 17th Bde RFA, 186th Bde RFA and 3rd Army Reinforcement Camp × The officers being posted as follows: Capt A. Wale posted to 186 Bde RFA. 2/Lt A.J. Applegate posted to 17th Bde RFA 2/Lt E.J. Brown posted to 17th Bde RFA 2/Lt R.L. Close posted to No 2 Section 39 DAC 2/Lt J.C. Green posted to 186 Bde RFA Capt. J. Mulligan RFA and Special Detachment on Act: are in MYENVILLE Sub-Sector for a trial shoot in the line with the 6" Mobile (Manned) Trench Mortar	Officers of X/39 MTM Bty Officers of Y/39 MTM Bty
	16th		(Capt J.A. Procter Exempted dist: posted to Infantry Base Depot (Notts & Derby Regt)	
	17th		7/Lt P.R. Andrews F/C Essex Regt posted to Infantry Base Depot (1 Herts Regt)	

39° Dv. T M Battery

WAR DIARY
for
INTELLIGENCE SUMMARY

May 1919 (cont)

Army Form C. 2118.

Place	Date	Hour	Summary of Events and Information	Remarks and references to Appendices
	18th		Capt. T. Mulligan, RFA and Special Detachment in action on "Boistraux St Marc" sub sector, in another trial about with the 6" Mobile mounted Trench Mortar.	

J Mulligan
Capt. RFA
D.T.M.O.
39 RFA

WAR DIARY or INTELLIGENCE SUMMARY

Army Form C. 2118

39D TM Bty
Vol. 29.
1 - 31 JULY 1918.

Place	Date	Hour	Summary of Events and Information	Remarks and references to Appendices
ST. LEGER	2nd		25 K B.de took over lines on relief. N.D. 1 & 2 Sections marched to DOULLENS and MONDICOURT and entrained for 2nd Army Area.	
DROGLANDT	3rd		N.D. & C Section detrained at PROVEN & REXPOEDE and marched to DROOGLANDT Area. N.B. N.D.O.16.	
ST. JAN TER BIEZEN	18	9pm	No 2 Section came under fire of 33" SW. Fos ot No 1 Section E 27 a 88. Shell 27. B26 took over 2 site for Gun Dumps and Fuse Dumps at F 27 & 85 and 23 & 25. Shell 27.	
	19	3.30 am	No 2 Section moved to F 27 & 85. Shell 27.	
	20		Work was commenced on the Right section Gun Position of K End Group system.	
	23		14000 4 YDX v 3600 B.X. was taken up by tram to DAWSON and dumped in the forward area gun positions.	

W Cooper
2/Lt RFA
Comdg 39D TM Bty